WEST CHICAGO PUBLIC LIBRARY DISTRICT   2 l

3 6058 00283 8   P9-DHT-075

West Chicago Public Library **District**
118 West Washington
West Chicago, IL 60185-2803
Phone # (630) 231-1552
Fax # (630) 231-1709

TEAM SPORTS
OF THE
SUMMER GAMES

Aaron Derr

RED CHAIR
·PRESS·

Gold Medal Games is produced and published by Red Chair Press:

Red Chair Press LLC   PO Box 333   South Egremont, MA 01258-0333
www.redchairpress.com

Publisher's Cataloging-In-Publication Data

Names: Derr, Aaron, author. | Sperling, Thomas, 1952- illustrator.

Title: Team sports of the Summer Games / Aaron Derr ; [illustrations by
    Thomas Sperling].

Description: South Egremont, MA : Red Chair Press, [2020] | Series: Gold
    medal games | Interest age level: 007-010. | Includes bibliographical
    references and index. | Summary: "An overview of the modern Olympic
    Games featuring sports played by teams of athletes competing against
    each other ... The games showcase the strength and skills, stamina and
    endurance of amazing athletic teams from around the world in a show of
    sportsmanship."--Provided by publisher.

Identifiers: ISBN 9781634407229 (library hardcover) | ISBN 9781634407274
    (paperback) | ISBN 9781634407328 (ebook)

Subjects: LCSH: Olympics--Juvenile literature. | Team sports--Juvenile
    literature. | CYAC: Olympics. | Sports.

Classification: LCC GV721.53 .D472 2020 (print) | LCC GV721.53 (ebook) |
    DDC 796.48--dc23

LCCN: 2018963385

Copyright © 2020 Red Chair Press LLC
RED CHAIR PRESS, the RED CHAIR and associated logos are registered
trademarks of Red Chair Press LLC.

All rights reserved. No part of this book may be reproduced, stored in an
information or retrieval system, or transmitted in any form by any means,
electronic, mechanical including photocopying, recording, or otherwise
without the prior written permission from the Publisher. For permissions,
contact info@redchairpress.com

Illustrations by Thomas Sperling.

Photo credits: Cover, pp. 1–5, 7 (bottom), 8 (bottom), 11–17, 21, 22, 23 (top),
24–32, 33 (left), 35 (bottom), 36, 38–39, 40, 42 45 Shutterstock; p. 6 © AF
archive/Alamy; p. 7 (top) © Bob Thomas/Popperfoto/Getty Images; pp. 8 (top),
10, 23 (bottom) © PA Images/Alamy; p. 9 (top) © Topical Press Agency /Getty
Images; pp. 9 (bottom), 37 © ZUMA Press, Inc. /Alamy; pp. 18, 19 © Neil
Leifer/Getty Images; p. 33 (right) © Action Plus Sports Images /Alamy; p. 34
© Everett Collection, Inc /Alamy; pp. 35 (top), 39, 43 © dpa picture alliance /
Alamy; p. 41 © Xinhua /Alamy; p. 44 © PCN Photography/Alamy.

Printed in the United States of America

0619 1P CGS20

TABLE OF CONTENTS

CHAPTER 1

TEAM SPORTS AT THE SUMMER GAMES

Remains of the ancient Olympic stadium can still be found today in Olympia, Greece.

The **ancient** Olympic Games began more than 2,500 years ago, lasted more than 500 years, and included all kinds of fascinating events.

There was a running event called the stade*. For many years, it was the only event at the Olympics! Later, there was horse racing, **chariot** racing, wrestling and boxing.

* The stade was a foot race like a sprint.

But one thing the ancient Olympics never had was team sports. When the Olympics were permanently canceled in 393 AD, it seemed as if there would never be any team sports in the Olympics!

But after a 2,000-year break, the Olympics made a comeback. The first **modern** Olympic Games were held in Athens, Greece, in 1896. They featured 43 different events, including track and field, gymnastics, swimming, and much more. But still, there were no team sports.

A scene from the television miniseries
The First Olympics: Athens 1896

The rugby team from France won the Gold medal in 1900.

All of that changed four years later. In the 1900 Summer Olympics, held in Paris, France, there were new team sports: soccer, water polo and rugby. Finally!

FYI

A new form of basketball is coming to the Olympics in 2020. It's called 3X3 because there are only three players per side.

Water polo is a game that's a lot like soccer, except it's played in a swimming pool. It has been included in every single Summer

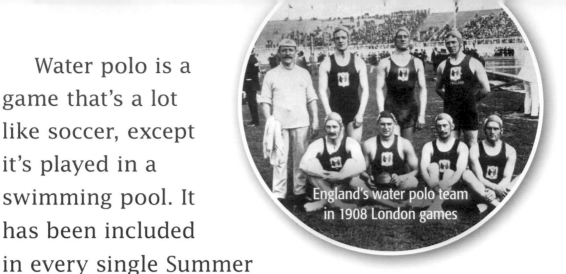

England's water polo team in 1908 London games

Olympics since 1900. Soccer has been included in every Summer Games since then as well, except for 1932, when it took a one-year break.

Water polo is one of the most popular team sports in the Summer Games.

Field hockey, 1908 London games

In 1908, field hockey was added to the official Olympic program. Field hockey is similar to ice hockey, except it's played on a field like soccer. No ice skating necessary!

Great Britain versus Netherlands, Rio de Janeiro 2016

Basketball in Berlin, 1936, Philippines vs Mexico

Then, in 1936, the Olympics added handball and basketball. Handball is another game like soccer, except you get to use your hands. It was played outdoors at just one Olympics before being dropped for 36 years.

In 1972, handball returned, only this time they played indoors. Indoor handball is the most popular version of the game today.

Handball in Rio de Janeiro, 2016

From Rivals to Teammates

Volleyball was added to the Summer Games in 1964. Six players on each team try to hit—or volley—the ball over a net. They play in an indoor arena.

In 1992, a new version of volleyball burst onto the scene: beach volleyball! They don't actually play on the beach. Teams of two players each play the sport outdoors on the sand.

Beach volleyball in Rio, 2016, Brazil vs Russia

FYI
Both baseball and softball return to the Summer Games in 2020. The last time they were official Olympic sports was in 2008. Welcome back!

The most recent addition to the list of team sports at the Olympics is rugby. Also known as rugby football, rugby is a sport in which teams work together to try to run with a ball down the field while players from the other team try to tackle them. Ouch!

It was played for the first time in the 2016 Games. The Olympic version is officially called rugby sevens because there are seven players per side. There are other versions of rugby that include 15, 13, 10 or six players.

Team sports at the Olympics are unique because players who normally play on different teams get to play together. Some of the biggest **rivals** in basketball, soccer and other sports put their differences aside every four years to play for their countries in the Olympics!

Rugby in Rio, 2016, Brazil vs Kenya

Rio de Janeiro's Maracana Stadium

Gold Medal Cities

The Summer Olympics are hosted by a different city every four years. Here is a list of the host cities for the past Summer Games, plus some that haven't even happened yet. The IOC really likes to plan ahead!

2028: Los Angeles	2004: Athens	1980: Moscow
2024: Paris	2000: Sydney	1976: Montreal
2020: Tokyo	1996: Atlanta	1972: Munich
2016: Rio de Janeiro	1992: Barcelona	1968: Mexico
2012: London	1988: Seoul	1964: Tokyo
2008: Beijing	1984: Los Angeles	1960: Rome

BASKETBALL
AND SOCCER

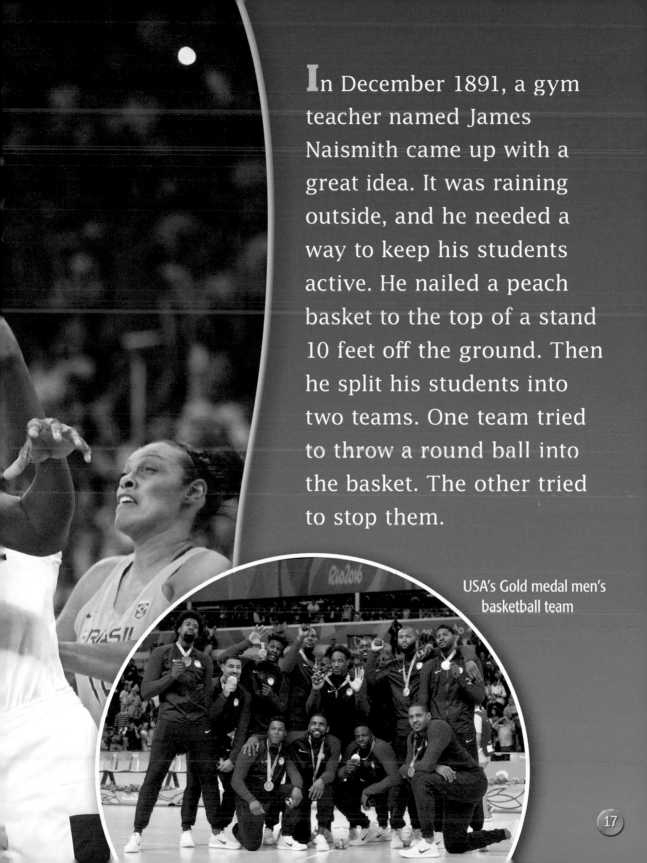

In December 1891, a gym teacher named James Naismith came up with a great idea. It was raining outside, and he needed a way to keep his students active. He nailed a peach basket to the top of a stand 10 feet off the ground. Then he split his students into two teams. One team tried to throw a round ball into the basket. The other tried to stop them.

USA's Gold medal men's basketball team

Basketball was born!

Less than 50 years later, basketball was an official Olympic sport, and it has remained a part of the Games ever since. In fact, Dr. Naismith himself presented the medals at the 1936 Olympics.

No country has won more medals in basketball than the United States. From 1936 to 1968, the American men's team didn't lose a single game.

In 1992, players from the National Basketball Association (NBA) were allowed to play for their home countries in the Olympics. These are the best players in the world, and many of them are from the United States!

USA's mens team at awards ceremony, Barcelona, 1992

NBA players on the Gold medal team in 1992
(l to r) Larry Bird, Michael Jordan, Magic Johnson

The 1992 U.S. men's Olympic basketball team was called the Dream Team. Many fans think to this day it is the greatest sports team ever **assembled**.

The Dream Team featured some of the best men's basketball players of all time. Guys like Michael Jordan, Magic Johnson, Charles Barkley and Larry Bird. They won their games by an average of 44 points. They were unstoppable!

What a Dream!

People across the world were fascinated by the Dream Team. Players from other countries would ask the American players for their autographs after the games. Fans from other countries would cheer for the United States.

Many of the U.S. players were rivals when they played in the NBA. But when they played for Team USA, they were great teammates.

"I don't think there's anything better than representing your country," Barkley said. "I don't think anything in my life can come close to that."

In 1976, women were allowed to play basketball at the Olympics for the first time. The United States women are really good, too. They won every single game they played from 1996 to 2016.

JUST JOKING

Q: Why did the chicken cross the basketball court?

A: The referee was calling fowls!

Rio, 2016,
Argentina vs Australia

Soccer

Football is one of the most popular sports in the world. Not "American football" that you watch on Sundays in the fall. But football, the game where players are only allowed to touch the ball with their feet.

Brazil wins the Gold medal **match** vs Germany in Rio, 2016.

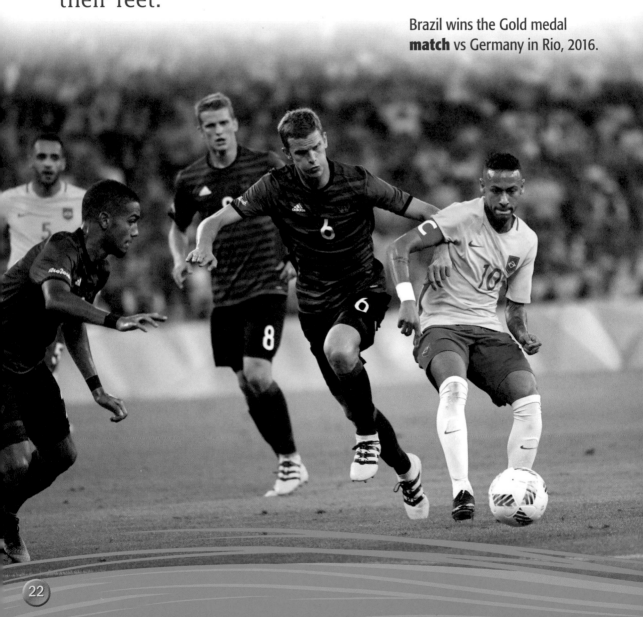

22

You might know it as soccer. But outside of the United States, it's called football. Most experts think the game goes all the way back to 200 BC in China, when men and women played a game call cuju. The rules were pretty much the same as modern soccer: players tried to kick the ball through an opening in a net. No hands allowed!

Soccer became an Olympic sport in 1900 and has been included every year since except for 1932.

Or Is It Football?

International soccer competition is different from other team sports in one big way: the **official** time is kept on the field by a **referee**, not on a giant scoreboard for everyone to see. Unlike in American football, when the clock stops for timeouts, injuries and television commercials, the clock in Olympic soccer runs continuously.

However, the referee may add time to the game when play stops for any reason. Near the end of each half, the referee signals how much stoppage time they will add. An official on the sideline then holds up a board that shows the fans how much time will be added.

A referee keeps the game under control.

Just like in basketball, soccer players in the Olympics might play alongside other players that they normally compete against. On the other hand, during the Olympics, a player might try to beat a player from another country who normally plays on his or her same team!

In addition to competing in the Olympics, many countries also compete in another international soccer **tournament** called the World Cup. The World Cup began in 1930 and is held every four years, just like the Olympics. The world just can't get enough soccer ... umm... football!

Superstar Cristiano Ronaldo played for Portugal in Athens, 2004.

VOLLEYBALL AND HANDBALL

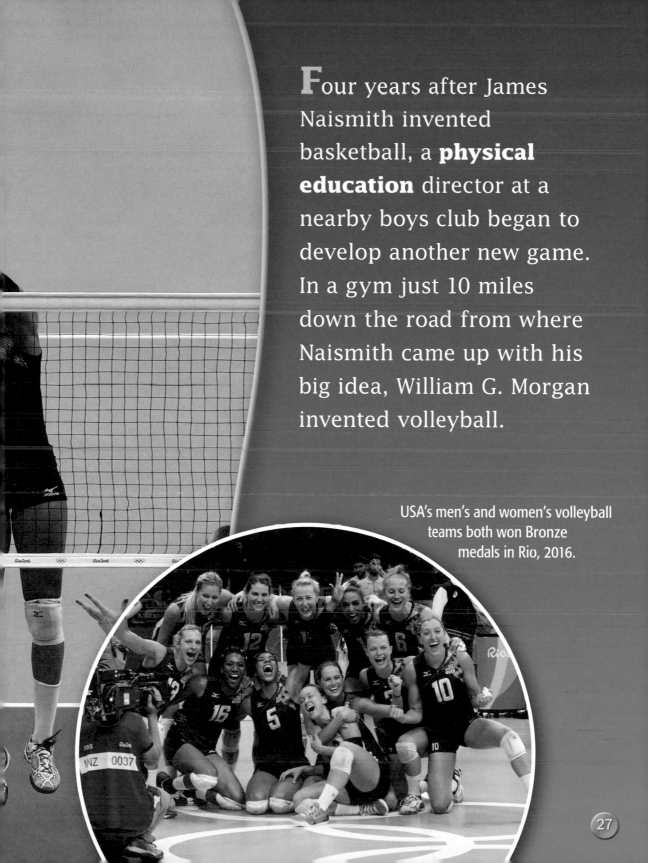

Four years after James Naismith invented basketball, a **physical education** director at a nearby boys club began to develop another new game. In a gym just 10 miles down the road from where Naismith came up with his big idea, William G. Morgan invented volleyball.

USA's men's and women's volleyball teams both won Bronze medals in Rio, 2016.

Practice Makes Perfect

Men and women volleyball players must practice six skills: serve, pass, set, attack, block and dig. The serve is the first play of each point. A player stands at the back of the **court** and hits the ball over the net. A successful serve is usually low and aimed at a spot on the other side of the net where no one is standing.

The pass is when the opposing team receives the serve. But they don't try to hit it back over the net right away! Instead, they try to pass it to a teammate. The pass is usually followed by a set, when a teammate sets up another teammate for an attack.

JUST JOKING

Q: What do you call a girl who stands in the middle of a volleyball court?

A: Annette!

No country **dominated** volleyball at the Olympics like the Soviet Union. Their men's and women's team earned six medals each. The Soviet Union was a group of states that existed until 1991. When it split into several different countries, its Olympic teams were split up, too.

Both men's and women's volleyball were added to the Summer Olympics in 1964. More than 30 years later, another version of volleyball was added: beach volleyball. The game is very similar to regular volleyball, except there are two players on a side instead of six.

And instead of playing on a court, beach volleyball is played on sand. This makes it easier for the players to dive for the ball and make all kinds of spectacular plays!

USA vs Netherlands, Rio, 2016

An attack, also called a spike, is when a player slams the ball over the net. If the ball crosses over the net and touches the ground, the team that knocked it over gets a point! That's why the receiving team will try to block the attack by jumping up right at the net. Or they might try to dig the ball by tapping it up right before it hits the ground.

Terrific Teammates

Two of the most successful beach volleyball players of all time are Americans Misty May-Treanor and Kerri Walsh Jennings. They won the gold medal in 2004, 2008 and 2012. No beach volleyballers have ever won more!

In fact, between the Olympics and other volleyball tournaments, May-Treanor and Jennings won 112 matches in a row before they finally retired from the sport. They were simply unstoppable!

Jennings (left), May-Treanor (right)

American women dominate beach volleyball.

In addition to being great teammates, the dynamic duo was also known for being great friends.

"It's very similar to a marriage or sisterhood," May-Treanor said. "We genuinely care for each other and we balance our lives on and off the court. When we get together, it's like we never left."

Gold medal winners, Beijing 2008
Jennings (left), May-Treanor (right)

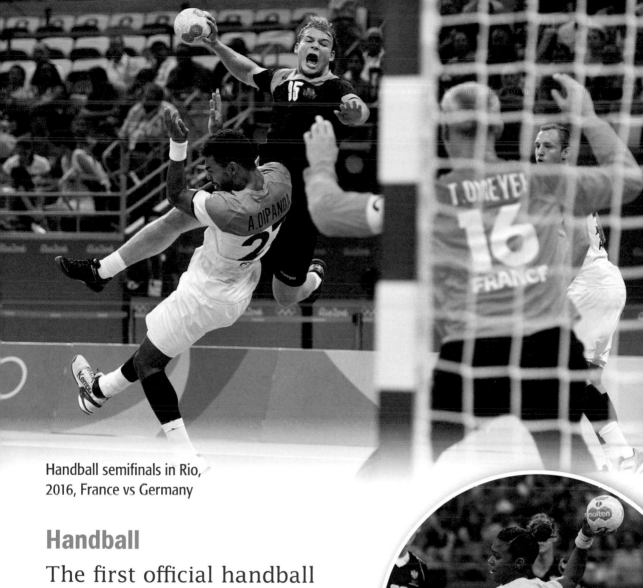

Handball semifinals in Rio, 2016, France vs Germany

Handball

The first official handball rules were published in Europe in 1906, but many historians think that games like handball were played thousands of years earlier in Rome, France and Greenland.

In modern handball, there are six players plus one **goalkeeper** per side. Like soccer, the six players must work together as a team to move the ball up the court. Instead of kicking the ball into the goal, handball players throw the ball into the goal.

Like basketball, handball players must dribble the ball when they move. But in basketball, players are allowed to take only one step without dribbling. In handball, they can take three steps. This leads to all kinds of fancy moves!

Goalkeepers are the only players allowed in the goal area. Just like in soccer, they are not allowed to leave the goal area with the ball in their hands. That means everyone has to work together to win the game!

Egypt vs Sweden, 2016, Rio. Handball is like soccer but using the hands!

Women's handball: Russia beats France to win Gold in Rio, 2016.

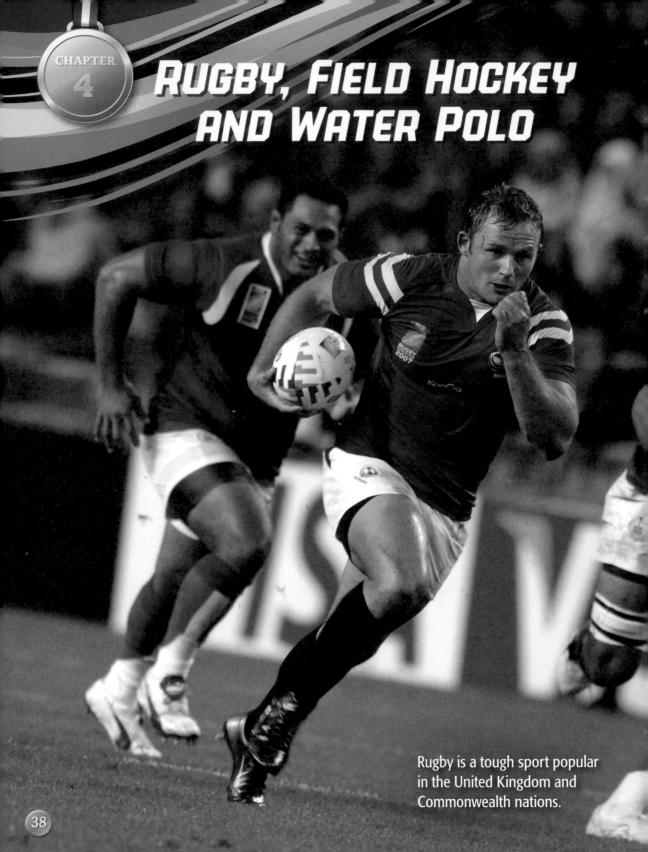

CHAPTER 4

RUGBY, FIELD HOCKEY AND WATER POLO

Rugby is a tough sport popular in the United Kingdom and Commonwealth nations.

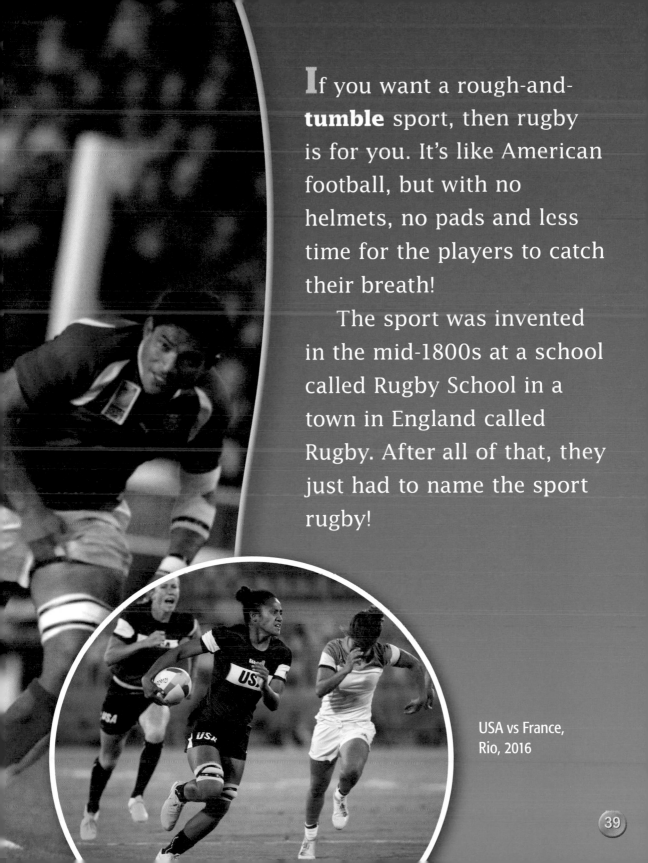

If you want a rough-and-**tumble** sport, then rugby is for you. It's like American football, but with no helmets, no pads and less time for the players to catch their breath!

The sport was invented in the mid-1800s at a school called Rugby School in a town in England called Rugby. After all of that, they just had to name the sport rugby!

USA vs France, Rio, 2016

JUST JOKING

Q: Why are dogs so annoying when they play rugby?

A: Because they're always roughing!

A rugby ball is similar to an American football except it's not quite as thin. There is no quarterback in rugby. In fact, there are no running backs, wide receivers or linemen. Everyone in rugby is the same!

Unlike in American football, in rugby the players can not throw the ball forward. A player can run forward with the ball until he is **tackled**, or he can kick the ball forward with the hopes that one his teammates can run and get it.

Just like in American football, the object of the game is to advance the ball across a **goal line** at each end of the field.

The Fiji men's rugby team won the gold medal in the 2016 Olympics, while the team from Australia won the women's medal. The United States actually won gold medals in rugby in both 1920 and 1924, when the sport was played with slightly different rules.

Women's rugby: Australia beats New Zealand 24–17 in Rio, 2016.

Field hockey is just like ice hockey but not as cold!

Field Hockey and Water Polo

Like rugby, field hockey was invented in England in the 1800s. By the time the 1908 Summer Olympics came around, the sport was popular enough to be included.

Field hockey players must move a small rolling ball down toward the goal using only their sticks. They aren't allowed to use their hands or kick the ball with their feet. Instead of trying to take the ball down the field by themselves, the best strategy is to pass the ball back and forth to your teammates. The teams that make the best passes usually win!

Men's field hockey, Argentina vs Netherlands, Rio 2016

Another fun Summer Olympics team sport is water polo. It's kind of like handball, except it's played in the water. Water polo players have to be super strong swimmers. The United States women's team has won the last two water polo gold medals.

"We are not Olympic champions because we woke up one day all on our own and did it," said Maggie Steffens, the captain of the team. "It takes an entire team, and years of preparation."

USA water polo captain Maggie Steffens

More Olympic Team Sports

There are a few other Olympic sports that might not officially be called team sports, but they still require more than one player to work together.

In **synchronized swimming**, up to eight swimmers perform a dance together in the water. All of the team members must move together at exactly the same time in order to get a good score from the judges.

Tennis is normally played with just one person on each side. However, tennis doubles features two players on each side working together. Badminton is similar to tennis doubles except the game is played on a much smaller court. Instead of hitting a ball, badminton players hit a shuttlecock, a cone-shaped object with a rubber bottom that bounces off the rackets.

There are tons of **sailing** events in the Olympics, and some of them include more than one person steering their boat to the finish line.

Even in the Olympic individual sports, there are **trainers** and coaches that work behind the scenes to help the players. Everywhere you look at the Olympics, people are working together to help their teams win!

GLOSSARY

ancient something that is very, very old

assembled something that has been put together, like a group of people

chariot a two-wheeled vehicle drawn by horses

court a surface used for playing a sport

dominate to be far and away the best at a sport

goal line the line at both ends of a sports playing field

goalkeeper the player who stays next to the goal for most of the game

match another word for game

modern something happened recently

official the final, authorized decision in a game or sport

physical education a class in which students learn about exercise and games

referee someone who make sure the players follow the rules

rivals people who compete against each other

tackle knocking a player to the ground

tournament a series of games in the same sport with multiple teams

trainer a person who helps athletes stay healthy

tumble to fall down

FOR MORE INFORMATION

Books About Olympians

McCallum, Jack. Dream Team: *How Michael, Magic, Larry, Charles, and the Greatest Team of All Time Conquered the World and Changed the Game of Basketball Forever.* Ballantine Books. 2012.

Lisa, Clemente. *The U.S. Women's Soccer Team: An American Success Story.* Scarecrow Press. 2010.

Christopher, Matt. *Great Moments in the Summer Olympics.* Little, Brown. 2012

May-Treanor, Misty. *Misty: Digging Deep in Volleyball and Life.* Simon and Schuster. 2010.

Places

United States Olympic Training Center, Colorado Springs, Colorado. Training center for Olympic athletes.

United States Olympic Training Center, San Diego, California. Another training center for Olympic athletes.

INDEX

ABOUT THE AUTHOR

Aaron Derr is a writer based just outside of Dallas, Texas. He has more than 15 years of experience as a writer and editor for magazines such as *Sports Illustrated for Kids*, *TIME for Kids*, and *Boys Life*. When he's not reading or writing, Aaron enjoys watching and playing sports, and doing pretty much anything with his wife and two kids.